The Standard Book of

Candle Magic

K.P. Theodore

Erebus Society

Erebus Society

First published in Great Britain in 2023
Erebus Society

First Edition

ISBN: 978-1-912461-52-3

www.ErebusSociety.com

Table of Contents

What is Candle Magic? 1

The Meaning of Colours...3

Preparing for Magical Practice..6

Casting the Circle..7

Tips..8

SPELLS..9

Ancestral Contact...10

Attraction 12

Awareness 14

Banishing...16

Banishment of Negative Thoughts and Feelings 18

Business Success 20

Calmness & Tranquility 22

Cleansing 24

Divination Ability Boost..26

Ease Stress and Anxiety...28

Emotional Healing 30

Focus and Concentration...32

Gratitude 34

Healing...36

Improve Memory..38

Intuition (to find)...40

Increase Intuition 42

Inspiration 44

Love 46

Manifestation 48

Meditation Aid 50

Mindfulness...52

Nightmare Prevention 54

Open the Third Eye..56

Past Trauma Relief 58

Positivity 60

Protection from Psychic Attack 62

Protection 64

Purification 66

Raise and Boost Energy 68

Relaxation 70

Romance 72

Soothing, Calm, and Peaceful Sleep 74

Spirit Contact 76

Success 78

Wealth 80

What is Candle Magic?

Candle magic, also known as candle magick, is a form of sympathetic magic that has been used in many cultures and traditions throughout history. The use of candles in magic can be traced back to ancient civilizations such as the Egyptians, Greeks, and Romans, who used candles in religious ceremonies and rituals. In many cultures, candles were used to honour the gods and goddesses and to bring blessings to the people.

In Wicca, candles are an essential part of many rituals and spells. They are used to represent the God and Goddess and to honour the elements of fire and light. They are also used to cast spells for love, prosperity, protection, and many other purposes. In Wicca, the colour of the candle, the scent of the candle, and the type of wax used are all believed to hold significance in the spell. For example, a red candle is often used in love spells, while a green candle is used in spells for wealth and abundance. Similarly, a yellow candle is used for spells involving knowledge and learning. Each colour of candle is believed to hold certain properties, which are taken into consideration when casting a spell.

Candles are also used in many rituals and ceremonies in Wicca. For example, a white candle is often used in rituals to represent the God and Goddess and to honour the elements of fire and light. A black candle is used to represent the element of earth and is often used in rituals involving protection and banishing. In addition to the colour, the scent of the candle also holds significance in Wicca. For example, a candle scented with lavender is believed to promote peace and tranquillity, while a candle scented with rose is believed to promote love and passion.

The use of candles in magic can also be found in hoodoo, a traditional African American system of magic that developed in the United States. In hoodoo, candles are used in a variety of spells and rituals such as love spells, money spells, and protection spells. They are often dressed with oils, herbs, and other magical items to enhance the energy of the spell. For example, a candle dressed with rose oil is believed to promote love and passion, while a candle dressed with cinnamon oil is believed to promote wealth and abundance.

In Christianity, candles have been used in religious rituals and ceremonies since ancient times. They are used to represent the light of Christ and to symbolize the presence of God. Candles are also used in many Catholic rituals such as the Rosary, the Vigil, and the Mass. For example, a candle is often lit in memory of a loved one who has passed away, or to symbolize the presence of the Holy Spirit.

Candle magic has also been used in many other cultures and traditions. It has been used in Taoist magic, in which candles are used to represent the elements of fire and light. It has been used in Native American spirituality, in which candles are used to honour the spirits of the ancestors.

The Meaning of Colours

Black:
Banishing and removing negative energy

Absorption of negative energy

Protection and secrecy

Blue:
Tranquillity and peace

Healing and protection

Communication and self-expression

Brown:
Stability and grounding

Connection to the Earth and nature

Finding and embracing one's roots and heritage

Gold:
Success and abundance

Attraction of wealth and prosperity

Connection to solar energies

Green:

Fertility and growth

Prosperity and abundance

Healing and balance

Orange:

Creativity and inspiration

Attraction of abundance and wealth

Encouragement of self-confidence and optimism

Pink:

Love and friendship

Emotional healing and nurturing

Inner peace and harmony

Purple:

Spirituality and psychic abilities

Ambition and success

Healing and protection

Red:

Passion and love

Strength and courage

Physical energy and vitality

Silver:

Intuition and psychic abilities

Protection and stability

Connection to the lunar energies

White:

Purity and innocence

Spiritual enlightenment and truth

Healing and protection

Yellow:

Intelligence and knowledge

Communication and divination

Attraction of good luck and happiness

Preparing for Magical Practice

When preparing to do magic, it is important to first tidy up the space you will be using. This can be done by cleaning and decluttering the area, and ensuring that it is free from distractions. This allows for a clear and focused mindset when performing your magic.

After tidying the space, it is important to cleanse the area in a magical way, such as with sage smudging. This helps to remove any negative energy or unwanted influences from the space and allows for a more powerful and effective magic.

Casting a magic circle of protection is an optional step, but it can be a useful way to create a sacred and protected space for your magic. This can be done by using a wand or athame to draw a circle around the area you will be working in, while visualizing the circle as a barrier that keeps out negative energy and unwanted influences.

Another optional step is to anoint the candles with magical oils. This can be done by using a small amount of oil on your finger and rubbing it onto the candle, while focusing on your intent and the properties of the oil. This helps to infuse the candle with your intent and the properties of the oil, making it more powerful for your magic.

Examples:

1. Tidy up your altar space by removing any clutter, dusting and cleaning, and lighting a nice smelling candle.

2. Smudge the room with sage to clear any negative energy before starting your spell.

3. Cast a circle of protection by walking around your altar space with a lit white candle, visualizing a bright white protective light surrounding you and your altar.

4. Anoint your candle with a drop of lavender oil to attract peace and tranquillity to your spell.

It is important to note that each tradition, coven and individual may have different ways of preparing for magic, these are just some examples. It's always best to follow your own intuition and the guidance of your tradition or teacher.

Casting the Circle

Casting a protection circle spell can be a powerful way to create a sacred space for ritual work or to shield yourself from negative energy. Here are the steps for casting a protection circle:

1. Prepare your space: Choose a quiet, private location where you will not be interrupted. Clear the area of any distractions or clutter. You may also want to cleanse the space with sage or another purifying herb.

2. Gather your supplies: You will need a candle, some incense, and a crystal or stone for grounding. You may also want to have a piece of paper and pen to write down any specific intentions or affirmations.

3. Set your intention: Before you begin, take a moment to connect with your intention for casting the protection circle. What do you hope to accomplish? What do you need to feel safe and protected?

4. Light the candle and incense: Hold the candle in your dominant hand and the incense in your other hand. Close your eyes and take a few deep breaths. When you feel centred and grounded, light the candle and incense.

5. Place the crystal or stone in the centre of the space: This will serve as the centre of your protection circle and will help to ground the energy of the spell.

6. Begin to cast the circle: You can use a tool such as an athame, wand, or your finger to trace a circle around the perimeter of the space. As you do this, say aloud or to yourself a phrase such as "I call upon the elements and the divine to create a protective circle around me."

7. Continue the spell: Once you have completed the circle, you can add any additional elements to the spell such as reciting a specific incantation or placing protective herbs or crystals around the perimeter.

8. Close the circle: When you are finished with the spell, thank the elements and the divine for their assistance and close the circle. You can do this by walking around the perimeter in a clockwise direction and saying a phrase such as "I release this circle and give thanks for its protection." Extinguish the candle and incense, and dispose of them safely.

Remember, spells and rituals are personal and can be adapted to your individual beliefs and practices. You may want to research different techniques and incorporate elements that resonate with you.

TIPS

- Choose the appropriate colour of candle for your intention. Each colour corresponds to different energies and properties, and can enhance the effectiveness of your spell.

- Anoint your candles with essential oils or herbs that correspond to your intention. This can add extra power to your spell and also make your space smell lovely.

- Set your intention clearly in your mind before lighting the candle. Visualize your desired outcome and focus on it while lighting the candle.

- Be mindful of the flame and never leave a burning candle unattended.

- Use a candle holder or heat-proof dish to catch any wax drippings.

- Keep your space clear of any flammable materials while working with candles.

- Dress your candle with symbols or words that correspond to your intention. This could be done by carving symbols into the wax, or by writing words on the candle with a permanent marker.

- Timing is important in candle magic. Choose the appropriate day and astrological timing for your spell.

- Trust in the power of the elements, the universe and the energy you are calling upon. Have faith that your spell will manifest.

- Always thank the elements and any spirit entities you have called upon after your spell is finished. Show gratitude for their assistance.

SPELLS

Ancestral Contact

Items needed:

- Brown candle
- Sandalwood or cedarwood oil
- Matches or a lighter
- A piece of jet or onyx
- A small bowl of dried rosemary or bay leaves

Instructions:

1. Cleanse your space by smudging with sage or burning lavender.

2. Sit comfortably in front of the candle and ground yourself by taking a few deep breaths.

3. Create a protective circle by casting rosemary or bay leaves around the area where you will be performing the spell.

4. Hold the jet or onyx in your hand, and visualise it connecting you with the energies of your ancestors.

5. Anoint the candle with sandalwood or cedarwood oil, starting at the wick and moving downward. As you do this, visualise yourself opening a communication channel with your ancestors.

6. Place the jet or onyx on the altar or nearby.

7. Light the candle and recite the following incantation:

By the power of the elements and the light of the ancestors, I call upon the spirits of my forefathers and foremothers. With the help of the jet/onyx and the rosemary/bay leaves, I invite my ancestors to come forward and communicate with me. With the use of sandalwood/cedarwood oil, I open my mind and senses to the guidance of my lineage. I trust in the universe to guide me and protect me in this communication.

It is important to remember that after the spell is cast, it is important to be open and receptive to any communication that may occur, and to have a way to end the communication when you are finished, such as saying thank you and closing the circle. Keep the jet or onyx near you to continue connecting you with the energies of your ancestors.

Attraction

Items needed:

- Orange candle
- Abundance oil (such as cinnamon or vanilla)
- Matches or a lighter
- A piece of citrine or tiger's eye
- A small bowl of honey

Instructions:

1. Cleanse your space by smudging with sage or burning lavender.

2. Sit comfortably in front of the candle and ground yourself by taking a few deep breaths.

3. Create a protective circle by casting a circle of honey around the area where you will be performing the spell.

4. Hold the citrine or tiger's eye in your hand, and visualise it absorbing the energy of abundance and manifestation.

5. Anoint the candle with abundance oil, starting at the wick and moving downward. As you do this, visualise yourself manifesting your desires and needs.

6. Place the citrine or tiger's eye on the altar or nearby.

7. Light the candle and recite the following incantation:

By the power of the elements and the light of the sun, I call upon the energies of attraction and manifestation. With the help of the citrine/tiger's eye and the abundance oil, I invite abundance and prosperity into my life. With the use of the honey, I sweeten my desires and needs. I trust in the universe to bring me what I need.

After the spell is cast, allow the candle to burn out completely and dispose of the used wax with respect and gratitude. Keep the citrine or tiger's eye near you to continue absorbing the energy of abundance and manifestation.

It's important to remember that the law of attraction is all about aligning your thoughts, emotions and actions to manifest your desires, so don't just rely on spells, but also work hard and have a positive attitude towards your goals and desires.

Awareness

Items needed:

- Yellow candle
- Lemon or peppermint oil
- Matches or a lighter
- A piece of citrine or yellow calcite
- A small bowl of dried lemon balm

Instructions:

1. Cleanse your space by smudging with sage or burning lavender.

2. Sit comfortably in front of the candle and ground yourself by taking a few deep breaths.

3. Create a protective circle by casting lemon balm around the area where you will be performing the spell.

4. Hold the citrine or yellow calcite in your hand, and visualise it absorbing the energy of awareness and understanding.

5. Anoint the candle with lemon or peppermint oil, starting at the wick and moving downward. As you do this, visualise yourself becoming more aware and understanding of yourself and the world around you.

6. Place the citrine or yellow calcite on the altar or nearby.

7. Light the candle and recite the following incantation:

By the power of the elements and the light of the sun, I call upon the energies of awareness and understanding. With the help of the citrine/yellow calcite and the lemon balm, I invite a heightened sense of awareness to guide me. With the use of lemon/peppermint oil, I open my mind and senses to the world around me. I trust in the universe to help me to see the truth and understand it.

After the spell is cast, allow the candle to burn out completely and dispose of the used wax with respect and gratitude. Keep the citrine or yellow calcite near you to continue absorbing the energy of awareness and understanding.

It is also important to maintain a consistent practice of self-reflection and understanding in everyday life. Additionally, surrounding yourself with knowledge, education and people that can help you to see different perspectives can help to promote a sense of awareness and understanding.

Banishing

Items needed:

- Black candle
- Dragon's blood or banishing oil
- Matches or a lighter
- A piece of black tourmaline or onyx
- A piece of paper and pen
- Salt

Instructions:

1. Cleanse your space by smudging with sage or burning lavender.

2. Sit comfortably in front of the candle and ground yourself by taking a few deep breaths.

3. Draw a banishing symbol (such as a pentagram) on the piece of paper, and write the name of the person or energy you wish to banish on it.

4. Place the black tourmaline or onyx on top of the paper.

5. Anoint the candle with dragon's blood or banishing oil, starting at the wick and moving downward. As you do this, visualise the person or energy you wish to banish being pushed away from you.

6. Light the candle and recite the following incantation:

By the power of the elements and the light of the moon, I call upon the energies of banishing and protection. I banish (name of person or energy) from my life, Let them no longer hold power over me. With the help of black tourmaline/ onyx and the banishing oil, I create a barrier to protect me from any further harm. With the use of salt, I seal this banishing spell.

After the spell is cast, allow the candle to burn out completely and dispose of the used wax, paper and tourmaline/onyx with respect and gratitude, bury it in earth or throw it in running water.

Banishment of Negative Thoughts and Feelings

Items needed:

- Black candle
- Frankincense or myrrh oil
- Matches or a lighter
- A piece of obsidian or black tourmaline
- A small bowl of dried rosemary or sage

Instructions:

1. Cleanse your space by smudging with sage or burning lavender.

2. Sit comfortably in front of the candle and ground yourself by taking a few deep breaths.

3. Create a protective circle by casting rosemary or sage around the area where you will be performing the spell.

4. Hold the obsidian or black tourmaline in your hand, and visualise it absorbing and neutralizing any negative thoughts and feelings.

5. Anoint the candle with frankincense or myrrh oil, starting at the wick and moving downward. As you do this, visualise yourself banishing any negative thoughts and feelings.

6. Place the obsidian or black tourmaline on the altar or nearby.

7. Light the candle and recite the following incantation:

By the power of the elements and the light of the sun, I call upon the energies of banishment and purification. With the help of the obsidian/black tourmaline and the rosemary/sage, I invite the release of negative thoughts and feelings. With the use of frankincense/myrrh oil, I open my mind and senses to the power of positivity. I trust in the universe to guide me and support me in banishing negativity.

It is important to remember that after the spell is cast, it is important to continue to actively work on managing and releasing negative thoughts and feelings through healthy coping mechanisms such as therapy, mindfulness, and self-reflection. Keep the obsidian or black tourmaline near you to continue absorbing and neutralizing any negative energy.

Also, it's important to remember that true emotional well-being comes from within and it can be strengthened through self-discovery and understanding, rather than relying on external sources.

Business Success

Items needed:

- Green candle
- Peppermint or pine oil
- Matches or a lighter
- A piece of green aventurine or pyrite
- A small bowl of dried mint or basil

Instructions:

1. Cleanse your space by smudging with sage or burning lavender.

2. Sit comfortably in front of the candle and ground yourself by taking a few deep breaths.

3. Create a protective circle by casting mint or basil around the area where you will be performing the spell.

4. Hold the green aventurine or pyrite in your hand, and visualise it bringing abundance and prosperity to your business.

5. Anoint the candle with peppermint or pine oil, starting at the wick and moving downward. As you do this, visualise yourself manifesting success in your business.

6. Place the green aventurine or pyrite on the altar or nearby.

7. Light the candle and recite the following incantation:

By the power of the elements and the light of the sun, I call upon the energies of prosperity and success. With the help of the green aventurine/pyrite and the mint/basil, I invite abundance and growth in my business. With the use of peppermint/pine oil, I open my mind and senses to the opportunities for success. I trust in the universe to guide me and support me in my business ventures.

It is important to remember that after the spell is cast, it is important to be open and receptive to any opportunities that may arise, and to have a plan to make use of any success that may come your way. Keep the green aventurine or pyrite near you to continue bringing abundance and prosperity to your business.

Also it's important to remember, the success in business takes hard work, dedication, planning, and understanding of the market and competition.

Calmness & Tranquillity

Items needed:

- Blue candle
- Chamomile or lavender oil
- Matches or a lighter
- A piece of blue lace agate or aquamarine
- A small bowl of dried chamomile

Instructions:

1. Cleanse your space by smudging with sage or burning lavender.

2. Sit comfortably in front of the candle and ground yourself by taking a few deep breaths.

3. Create a protective circle by casting chamomile around the area where you will be performing the spell.

4. Hold the blue lace agate or aquamarine in your hand, and visualise it absorbing the energy of calm and tranquillity.

5. Anoint the candle with chamomile or lavender oil, starting at the wick and moving downward. As you do this, visualise yourself becoming more relaxed and at peace.

6. Place the blue lace agate or aquamarine on the altar or nearby.

7. Light the candle and recite the following incantation:

By the power of the elements and the light of the moon, I call upon the energies of calm and tranquillity. With the help of the blue lace agate/aquamarine and the chamomile, I invite peace and serenity into my mind and body. With the use of chamomile/lavender oil, I let go of stress and tension. I trust in the universe to bring me balance and harmony.

After the spell is cast, allow the candle to burn out completely and dispose of the used wax with respect and gratitude. Keep the blue lace agate or aquamarine near you to continue absorbing the energy of calm and tranquillity.

It's important to remember that this spell is not a replacement for self-care practices such as exercise, healthy eating, and getting enough sleep. It's a helpful tool to use in conjunction with other methods to promote relaxation and calm. Also, you can use this spell in combination with other practices such as meditation, yoga, deep breathing or listening to soothing music.

Cleansing

Items needed:

- White candle
- Sage or lavender essential oil
- Matches or a lighter
- A small bowl of sea salt
- A piece of rose quartz
- A feather
- A bowl of water

Instructions:

1. Cleanse your body by taking a purifying shower or bath, using sea salt and lavender or sage essential oil.

2. Cleanse your space by smudging with sage or burning lavender.

3. Sit comfortably in front of the altar and ground yourself by taking a few deep breaths.

4. Create a protective circle by casting salt around the altar and yourself.

5. Hold the rose quartz in your hand, and visualise it absorbing any negative energy or emotions that you wish to release.

6. Anoint the candle with sage or lavender oil, starting at the wick and moving downward. As you do this, visualise any negative energy or emotions being purified and released, and being absorbed by the rose quartz.

7. Place the rose quartz on the altar or nearby.

8. Light the candle and recite the following incantation:

By the power of the elements and the light of the moon, I call upon the energies of purification and release. I cleanse my body and my altar, Let all negativity be dissipated and let only positivity remain. With the help of the rose quartz and the sea salt, I create a barrier to protect me and my altar from any future negative influences. With the use of the feather and the water, I release these negative energies into the universe.

After the spell is cast, allow the candle to burn out completely and dispose of the used wax with respect and gratitude. Keep the rose quartz near you to continue absorbing any negative energy and protect you.

Divination Ability Boost

Items needed:

- Black candle
- Myrrh or frankincense oil
- Matches or a lighter
- A piece of obsidian or black onyx
- A small bowl of dried bay leaves

Instructions:

1. Cleanse your space by smudging with sage or burning lavender.

2. Sit comfortably in front of the candle and ground yourself by taking a few deep breaths.

3. Create a protective circle by casting bay leaves around the area where you will be performing the spell.

4. Hold the obsidian or black onyx in your hand, and visualise it absorbing the energy of divination and intuitive insight.

5. Anoint the candle with myrrh or frankincense oil, starting at the wick and moving downward. As you do this, visualise yourself becoming more attuned to your divination tools and intuition.

6. Place the obsidian or black onyx on the altar or nearby.

7. Light the candle and recite the following incantation:

By the power of the elements and the light of the moon, I call upon the energies of divination and intuitive insight. With the help of the obsidian/black onyx and the bay leaves, I invite the clarity and insight needed for divination. With the use of myrrh/frankincense oil, I open my mind and senses to receive guidance. I trust in the universe to reveal the truth.

After the spell is cast, allow the candle to burn out completely and dispose of the used wax with respect and gratitude. Keep the obsidian or black onyx near you to continue absorbing the energy of divination and intuitive insight.

It's important to remember that this spell is not a replacement for practice, study, and learning the techniques and methods of divination that you are interested in. This spell is a tool to help you be more open and receptive to the messages and guidance that you receive through your divination practices. Also, it's important to have a clear intention and focus when using your divination tools, and to be open and honest with yourself about what you hope to gain from the experience.

Ease Stress and Anxiety

Items needed:

- Green candle
- Eucalyptus or peppermint oil
- Matches or a lighter
- A piece of green aventurine or rose quartz
- A small bowl of dried lavender

Instructions:

1. Cleanse your space by smudging with sage or burning lavender.

2. Sit comfortably in front of the candle and ground yourself by taking a few deep breaths.

3. Create a protective circle by casting lavender around the area where you will be performing the spell.

4. Hold the green aventurine or rose quartz in your hand, and visualise it absorbing the energy of peace and calm.

5. Anoint the candle with eucalyptus or peppermint oil, starting at the wick and moving downward. As you do this, visualise yourself letting go of stress and anxiety.

6. Place the green aventurine or rose quartz on the altar or nearby.

7. Light the candle and recite the following incantation:

By the power of the elements and the light of the sun, I call upon the energies of peace and calm. With the help of the green aventurine/rose quartz and the lavender, I invite serenity and tranquility into my mind and body. With the use of eucalyptus/peppermint oil, I release stress and anxiety. I trust in the universe to bring me balance and harmony.

After the spell is cast, allow the candle to burn out completely and dispose of the used wax with respect and gratitude. Keep the green aventurine or rose quartz near you to continue absorbing the energy of peace and calm.

It's important to remember that this spell is not a replacement for self-care practices such as exercise, healthy eating, and getting enough sleep. It's a helpful tool to use in conjunction with other methods to promote relaxation and calm. Also, you can use this spell in combination with other practices such as meditation, yoga, deep breathing, journaling etc.

Emotional Healing

Items needed:

- Green candle
- Rose oil
- Matches or a lighter
- A piece of rose quartz
- A small bowl of dried rose petals

Instructions:

1. Cleanse your space by smudging with sage or burning lavender.

2. Sit comfortably in front of the candle and ground yourself by taking a few deep breaths.

3. Create a protective circle by casting rose petals around the area where you will be performing the spell.

4. Hold the rose quartz in your hand, and visualise it bringing love and healing to your emotions.

5. Anoint the candle with rose oil, starting at the wick and moving downward. As you do this, visualise yourself healing your emotional wounds.

6. Place the rose quartz on the altar or nearby.

7. Light the candle and recite the following incantation:

By the power of the elements and the light of the moon, I call upon the energies of love and healing. With the help of the rose quartz and the rose petals, I invite emotional healing into my life. With the use of rose oil, I open my heart to the power of self-love. I trust in the universe to guide me and support me in my emotional healing journey.

It is important to remember that after the spell is cast, emotional healing is a process that takes time and effort.

Remember that true healing comes from within, and it is important to take care of yourself and your emotional well-being.

Focus and Concentration

Items needed:

- Blue candle
- Rosemary or eucalyptus oil
- Matches or a lighter
- A piece of lapis lazuli or blue calcite
- A small bowl of dried rosemary

Instructions:

1. Cleanse your space by smudging with sage or burning lavender.

2. Sit comfortably in front of the candle and ground yourself by taking a few deep breaths.

3. Create a protective circle by casting rosemary around the area where you will be performing the spell.

4. Hold the lapis lazuli or blue calcite in your hand, and visualise it absorbing the energy of focus and concentration.

5. Anoint the candle with rosemary or eucalyptus oil, starting at the wick and moving downward. As you do this, visualise yourself becoming more focused and concentrated on your goals and tasks.

6. Place the lapis lazuli or blue calcite on the altar or nearby.

7. Light the candle and recite the following incantation:

By the power of the elements and the light of the sky, I call upon the energies of focus and concentration. With the help of the lapis lazuli/blue calcite and the rosemary, I invite a heightened sense of focus to guide me. With the use of rosemary/eucalyptus oil, I open my mind and senses to the task at hand. I trust in the universe to help me to achieve my goals with precision and determination.

After the spell is cast, allow the candle to burn out completely and dispose of the used wax with respect and gratitude. Keep the lapis lazuli or blue calcite near you to continue absorbing the energy of focus and concentration.

It's important to remember that this spell is not a replacement for daily practice of focus and concentration like creating a schedule, breaking down big tasks into smaller ones, eliminating distractions or taking short breaks, and practising mindfulness and meditation.

Gratitude

Items needed:

- Green candle
- Clove or cinnamon oil
- Matches or a lighter
- A piece of peridot or green aventurine
- A small bowl of dried rosemary

Instructions:

1. Cleanse your space by smudging with sage or burning lavender.

2. Sit comfortably in front of the candle and ground yourself by taking a few deep breaths.

3. Create a protective circle by casting rosemary around the area where you will be performing the spell.

4. Hold the peridot or green aventurine in your hand, and visualise it absorbing the energy of gratitude and abundance.

5. Anoint the candle with clove or cinnamon oil, starting at the wick and moving downward. As you do this, visualise yourself filled with gratitude for all that you have in your life.

6. Place the peridot or green aventurine on the altar or nearby.

7. Light the candle and recite the following incantation:

By the power of the elements and the light of the earth, I call upon the energies of gratitude and abundance. With the help of the peridot/green aventurine and the rosemary, I invite a heart filled with gratitude for all that I have. With the use of clove/cinnamon oil, I ignite the fire of thankfulness in my soul. I trust in the universe to guide me towards a life of abundance and contentment.

After the spell is cast, allow the candle to burn out completely and dispose of the used wax with respect and gratitude. Keep the peridot or green aventurine near you to continue absorbing the energy of gratitude and abundance.

It's important to remember that this spell is not a replacement for daily practice of gratitude like keeping a gratitude journal, expressing thankfulness to others, and taking time to appreciate the small things in life. Also, practising mindfulness and being present in the moment can help to increase feelings of gratitude.

Healing

Items needed:

- Green candle
- Healing oil (such as lavender, rosemary, or lemon)
- Matches or a lighter
- A piece of rose quartz
- A small bowl of sea salt

Instructions:

1. Cleanse your space by smudging with sage or burning lavender.

2. Sit comfortably in front of the candle and ground yourself by taking a few deep breaths.

3. Create a protective circle by casting salt around the area where you will be performing the spell.

4. Hold the rose quartz in your hand, and visualise it absorbing any negative energy or emotions that you wish to release.

5. Anoint the candle with healing oil, starting at the wick and moving downward. As you do this, visualise any negative energy or emotions being purified and released, and being absorbed by the rose quartz.

6. Place the rose quartz on the altar or nearby.

7. Light the candle and recite the following incantation:

By the power of the elements and the light of the moon, I call upon the energies of healing and rejuvenation. Let all negativity be dissipated and let only positivity remain. With the help of the rose quartz and the sea salt, I create a barrier to protect me from any future negative influences. With the use of the healing oil, I invite the healing energy to flow through me and my loved ones.

After the spell is cast, allow the candle to burn out completely and dispose of the used wax with respect and gratitude. Keep the rose quartz near you to continue absorbing any negative energy and protect you.

It's important to remember that spell casting is not a substitute for professional medical or psychological treatment.

It is also important to remember that the healing energy should be directed not only to oneself but also to others, in this way the healing spell can bring a positive change not only to the individual but also to the community.

Improve Memory

Items needed:

- Green candle
- Rosemary or peppermint oil
- Matches or a lighter
- A piece of green aventurine or moss agate
- A small bowl of dried rosemary

Instructions:

1. Cleanse your space by smudging with sage or burning lavender.

2. Sit comfortably in front of the candle and ground yourself by taking a few deep breaths.

3. Create a protective circle by casting rosemary around the area where you will be performing the spell.

4. Hold the green aventurine or moss agate in your hand, and visualise it absorbing the energy of memory and retention.

5. Anoint the candle with rosemary or peppermint oil, starting at the wick and moving downward. As you do this, visualise yourself becoming more capable of retaining and recalling information.

6. Place the green aventurine or moss agate on the altar or nearby.

7. Light the candle and recite the following incantation:

By the power of the elements and the light of the earth, I call upon the energies of memory and retention. With the help of the green aventurine/moss agate and the rosemary, I invite a sharp mind and clear memory to guide me. With the use of rosemary/peppermint oil, I open my mind and senses to the knowledge I seek. I trust in the universe to help me to remember and retain all that is important to me.

After the spell is cast, allow the candle to burn out completely and dispose of the used wax with respect and gratitude. Keep the green aventurine or moss agate near you to continue absorbing the energy of memory and retention.

It's important to remember that this spell is not a replacement for daily practice of memory improvement like mental exercises, repetition, and other memory-enhancing techniques.

Intuition (to find)

Items needed:

- Purple candle
- Mugwort or lavender oil
- Matches or a lighter
- A piece of amethyst
- A small bowl of dried mugwort

Instructions:

1. Cleanse your space by smudging with sage or burning lavender.

2. Sit comfortably in front of the candle and ground yourself by taking a few deep breaths.

3. Create a protective circle by casting mugwort around the area where you will be performing the spell.

4. Hold the amethyst in your hand, and visualise it absorbing the energy of intuition and psychic abilities.

5. Anoint the candle with mugwort or lavender oil, starting at the wick and moving downward. As you do this, visualise yourself becoming more in tune with your intuition and inner voice.

6. Place the amethyst on the altar or nearby.

7. Light the candle and recite the following incantation:

By the power of the elements and the light of the moon, I call upon the energies of intuition and psychic abilities. With the help of the amethyst and the mugwort, I invite intuition and inner knowledge to guide me. With the use of mugwort/lavender oil, I open my mind and senses to receive guidance. I trust in the universe to reveal my path.

After the spell is cast, allow the candle to burn out completely and dispose of the used wax with respect and gratitude. Keep the amethyst near you to continue absorbing the energy of intuition and psychic abilities.

It's important to remember that intuition spell is a tool to help you to listen to yourself and your inner voice, but it's not a replacement for critical thinking and decision making. Also, practising meditation, journaling, and connecting with nature can also help to increase your intuition and psychic abilities, as well as other practices such as dream journaling, tarot reading, and energy work.

Keep in mind that developing your intuition is a journey and it takes time and patience, so be kind and patient with yourself. Also, it's important to trust in your intuition and inner guidance, but always use your own judgement and common sense when making decisions.

Increase Intuition

Items needed:

- Purple candle
- Rosemary oil
- Matches or a lighter
- A piece of moonstone
- A small bowl of dried rosemary

Instructions:

1. Cleanse your space by smudging with sage or burning lavender.

2. Sit comfortably in front of the candle and ground yourself by taking a few deep breaths.

3. Create a protective circle by casting rosemary around the area where you will be performing the spell.

4. Hold the moonstone in your hand, and visualise it bringing clarity and insight to your mind and body.

5. Anoint the candle with rosemary oil, starting at the wick and moving downward. As you do this, visualise yourself opening your mind and senses to the intuitive messages of the universe.

6. Place the moonstone on the altar or nearby.

7. Light the candle and recite the following incantation:

By the power of the elements and the light of the moon, I call upon the energies of intuition and insight. With the help of the moonstone and the rosemary, I invite an increase in my intuitive abilities. With the use of rosemary oil, I open my mind and senses to the messages of the universe. I trust in the universe to guide me and support me in my journey to understanding.

Inspiration

Items needed:

- Blue candle
- Jasmine or lavender oil
- Matches or a lighter
- A piece of aquamarine or turquoise
- A small bowl of dried rose petals

Instructions:

1. Cleanse your space by smudging with sage or burning lavender.

2. Sit comfortably in front of the candle and ground yourself by taking a few deep breaths.

3. Create a protective circle by casting rose petals around the area where you will be performing the spell.

4. Hold the aquamarine or turquoise in your hand, and visualise it absorbing the energy of inspiration and creativity.

5. Anoint the candle with jasmine or lavender oil, starting at the wick and moving downward. As you do this, visualise yourself becoming filled with inspiration and ideas.

6. Place the aquamarine or turquoise on the altar or nearby.

7. Light the candle and recite the following incantation:

By the power of the elements and the light of the stars, I call upon the energies of inspiration and creativity. With the help of the aquamarine/turquoise and the rose petals, I invite a flow of ideas and inspiration to guide me. With the use of jasmine/lavender oil, I open my mind and senses to receive guidance. I trust in the universe to guide me towards my true purpose.

After the spell is cast, allow the candle to burn out completely and dispose of the used wax with respect and gratitude. Keep the aquamarine or turquoise near you to continue absorbing the energy of inspiration and creativity.

It's important to remember that this spell is not a replacement for self-exploration and creative practices, it's a tool to help you to align your energy and focus towards finding inspiration. Also, practising mindfulness and self-reflection, surrounding yourself with inspiration and taking time to pursue your creative passions are some of the ways to find inspiration.

Love

Items needed:

- Pink candle
- Rose oil or jasmine oil
- Matches or a lighter
- A piece of rose quartz
- A small bowl of rose petals

Instructions:

1. Cleanse your space by smudging with sage or burning lavender.

2. Sit comfortably in front of the candle and ground yourself by taking a few deep breaths.

3. Create a protective circle by casting rose petals around the area where you will be performing the spell.

4. Hold the rose quartz in your hand, and visualise it absorbing the energy of love and attraction.

5. Anoint the candle with rose or jasmine oil, starting at the wick and moving downward. As you do this, visualise yourself surrounded by love and positivity.

6. Place the rose quartz on the altar or nearby.

7. Light the candle and recite the following incantation:

By the power of the elements and the light of the moon, I call upon the energies of love and attraction. With the help of the rose quartz and the rose petals, I invite love and positivity into my life. With the use of rose/jasmine oil, I open my heart to receive love. I trust in the universe to bring me the love that I need.

After the spell is cast, allow the candle to burn out completely and dispose of the used wax with respect and gratitude. Keep the rose quartz near you to continue absorbing the energy of love and attraction.

It's important to remember that love spell should not be used to control others or manipulate their feelings. The goal of this spell is to open yourself to the possibility of love and positivity, not to force someone else to love you. Love should be given and received freely and with mutual respect and consent. Also, it's important to remember that this spell is not a quick fix, it will take time and effort on your part to manifest love in your life. It's important to work on yourself, improve yourself, be kind and open to others and have a positive attitude.

Additionally, you can use this spell to attract love, but keep in mind that it's not only about romantic love, but also love in all its forms, such as self-love, love for family, friends, and community.

Manifestation

Items needed:

- Yellow candle
- Orange or cinnamon oil
- Matches or a lighter
- A piece of citrine or pyrite
- A small bowl of dried basil

Instructions:

1. Cleanse your space by smudging with sage or burning lavender.

2. Sit comfortably in front of the candle and ground yourself by taking a few deep breaths.

3. Create a protective circle by casting basil around the area where you will be performing the spell.

4. Hold the citrine or pyrite in your hand, and visualise it absorbing the energy of manifestation and abundance.

5. Anoint the candle with orange or cinnamon oil, starting at the wick and moving downward. As you do this, visualise yourself manifesting your desires and goals.

6. Place the citrine or pyrite on the altar or nearby.

7. Light the candle and recite the following incantation:

By the power of the elements and the light of the sun, I call upon the energies of manifestation and abundance. With the help of the citrine/pyrite and the basil, I invite prosperity and success in all areas of my life. With the use of orange/cinnamon oil, I ignite the fire of my desires and set my intentions into motion. I trust in the universe to bring my goals to fruition.

After the spell is cast, allow the candle to burn out completely and dispose of the used wax with respect and gratitude. Keep the citrine or pyrite near you to continue absorbing the energy of manifestation and abundance.

It's important to remember that this spell is not a replacement for hard work and taking action towards your goals, it's a tool to help you to align your energy and focus towards your manifestation. Also, having a clear and specific intention and visualizing your desire, writing it down and taking action to achieve it, is important to make manifestation happen.

Meditation Aid

Items needed:

- Blue candle
- Sandalwood or lavender oil
- Matches or a lighter
- A piece of blue sapphire or lapis lazuli
- A small bowl of dried lavender or chamomile

Instructions:

1. Cleanse your space by smudging with sage or burning lavender.

2. Sit comfortably in front of the candle and ground yourself by taking a few deep breaths.

3. Create a protective circle by casting lavender or chamomile around the area where you will be performing the spell.

4. Hold the blue sapphire or lapis lazuli in your hand, and visualise it bringing peace and clarity to your meditation.

5. Anoint the candle with sandalwood or lavender oil, starting at the wick and moving downward. As you do this, visualise yourself achieving a deeper state of meditation.

6. Place the blue sapphire or lapis lazuli on the altar or nearby.

7. Light the candle and recite the following incantation:

By the power of the elements and the light of the sun, I call upon the energies of tranquillity and insight. With the help of the blue sapphire/lapis lazuli and the lavender/chamomile, I invite a deeper state of meditation. With the use of sandalwood/lavender oil, I open my mind and senses to the power of inner peace. I trust in the universe to guide me and support me in my meditation journey.

It is important to remember that after the spell is cast, it is important to continue to actively practice meditation and make it a regular part of your routine. Keep the blue sapphire or lapis lazuli near you to continue to bring peace and clarity to your meditation.

Also, it's important to remember that true meditative ability comes from within and can be strengthened through consistent practice and guidance, rather than relying on external sources.

Additionally, it may be helpful to research different meditation techniques, such as mindfulness, transcendental, and guided meditation, to find one that resonates with you. And always remember, like any skill, meditation takes time and consistent practice to improve.

Mindfulness

Items needed:

- White candle
- Frankincense or sandalwood oil
- Matches or a lighter
- A piece of clear quartz or white selenite
- A small bowl of dried lavender

Instructions:

1. Cleanse your space by smudging with sage or burning lavender.

2. Sit comfortably in front of the candle and ground yourself by taking a few deep breaths.

3. Create a protective circle by casting lavender around the area where you will be performing the spell.

4. Hold the clear quartz or white selenite in your hand, and visualise it absorbing the energy of mindfulness and clarity.

5. Anoint the candle with frankincense or sandalwood oil, starting at the wick and moving downward. As you do this, visualise yourself becoming more mindful and present in each moment.

6. Place the clear quartz or white selenite on the altar or nearby.

7. Light the candle and recite the following incantation:

By the power of the elements and the light within, I call upon the energies of mindfulness and clarity. With the help of the clear quartz/white selenite and the lavender, I invite a sense of calm and presence to guide me. With the use of frankincense/sandalwood oil, I open my mind and senses to the present moment. I trust in the universe to help me to find peace and mindfulness.

After the spell is cast, allow the candle to burn out completely and dispose of the used wax with respect and gratitude. Keep the clear quartz or white selenite near you to continue absorbing the energy of mindfulness and clarity.

It's important to remember that this spell is not a replacement for daily practice of mindfulness like meditation, yoga, or other forms of self-reflection. It is also important to maintain a consistent practice of mindfulness and self-awareness in everyday life. Additionally, surrounding yourself with calming and peaceful surroundings can help to promote a sense of mindfulness and presence in the moment.

Nightmare Prevention

Items needed:

- Blue candle
- Lavender oil
- Matches or a lighter
- A piece of amethyst
- A small bowl of dried lavender

Instructions:

1. Cleanse your space by smudging with sage or burning lavender.

2. Sit comfortably in front of the candle and ground yourself by taking a few deep breaths.

3. Create a protective circle by casting lavender around the area where you will be performing the spell.

4. Hold the amethyst in your hand, and visualise it bringing peace and protection to your dreams.

5. Anoint the candle with lavender oil, starting at the wick and moving downward. As you do this, visualise yourself banishing nightmares and negative dreams.

6. Place the amethyst on the altar or nearby.

7. Light the candle and recite the following incantation:

By the power of the elements and the light of the moon, I call upon the energies of peace and protection. With the help of the amethyst and the lavender, I invite peaceful dreams into my life. With the use of lavender oil, I banish nightmares and negative dreams. I trust in the universe to guide me and support me in my journey to peaceful sleep.

It is important to remember that after the spell is cast, preventing nightmares is a process that takes time and effort.

Remember that true peaceful sleep comes from within, and it is important to take care of yourself and your emotional well-being, practising good sleep hygiene and stress management techniques can also help with preventing nightmares.

Open the Third Eye

Items needed:

- Indigo candle
- Mugwort or pine oil
- Matches or a lighter
- A piece of sodalite or lapis lazuli
- A small bowl of dried mugwort

Instructions:

1. Cleanse your space by smudging with sage or burning lavender.

2. Sit comfortably in front of the candle and ground yourself by taking a few deep breaths.

3. Create a protective circle by casting mugwort around the area where you will be performing the spell.

4. Hold the sodalite or lapis lazuli in your hand, and visualise it absorbing the energy of intuition and psychic abilities.

5. Anoint the candle with mugwort or pine oil, starting at the wick and moving downward. As you do this, visualise yourself opening your third eye and becoming more in tune with your intuition and inner voice.

6. Place the sodalite or lapis lazuli on the altar or nearby.

7. Light the candle and recite the following incantation:

By the power of the elements and the light of the moon, I call upon the energies of intuition and psychic abilities. With the help of the sodalite/lapis lazuli and the mugwort, I invite the opening of my third eye and the revelation of hidden knowledge. With the use of mugwort/pine oil, I open my mind and senses to receive guidance. I trust in the universe to reveal my path.

After the spell is cast, allow the candle to burn out completely and dispose of the used wax with respect and gratitude. Keep the sodalite or lapis lazuli near you to continue absorbing the energy of intuition and psychic abilities.

It's important to remember that this spell is not a replacement for critical thinking and decision making, and it's not a guarantee that you will have psychic abilities, it's a tool to help you to listen to yourself and your inner voice. Also, practising meditation, journaling, and connecting with nature can also help to develop your intuition and psychic abilities.

Past Trauma Relief

Items needed:

- Blue candle
- Lavender oil
- Matches or a lighter
- A piece of amethyst
- A small bowl of dried lavender

Instructions:

1. Cleanse your space by smudging with sage or burning lavender.

2. Sit comfortably in front of the candle and ground yourself by taking a few deep breaths.

3. Create a protective circle by casting lavender around the area where you will be performing the spell.

4. Hold the amethyst in your hand, and visualise it bringing peace and calm to your mind and body.

5. Anoint the candle with lavender oil, starting at the wick and moving downward. As you do this, visualise yourself releasing the trauma and letting go of any negative emotions associated with it.

6. Place the amethyst on the altar or nearby.

7. Light the candle and recite the following incantation:

By the power of the elements and the light of the moon, I call upon the energies of healing and peace. With the help of the amethyst and the lavender, I invite release from past trauma. With the use of lavender oil, I release negative emotions and memories. I trust in the universe to guide me and support me in my journey to healing.

It's important to remember that healing from trauma is a process that takes time and effort.

Also, it's important to seek professional help, such as therapy or counselling, if you have difficulties to heal from past trauma or if you have trauma-related health issues. Remember that the spell is not a substitute for professional help and that self-care and mindfulness practices such as yoga, meditation, and exercise can also be beneficial in promoting healing.

Positivity

Items needed:

- Yellow candle
- Citrus oil (such as lemon, orange or grapefruit)
- Matches or a lighter
- A piece of clear quartz
- A small bowl of dried rose petals

Instructions:

1. Cleanse your space by smudging with sage or burning lavender.

2. Sit comfortably in front of the candle and ground yourself by taking a few deep breaths.

3. Create a protective circle by casting rose petals around the area where you will be performing the spell.

4. Hold the clear quartz in your hand, and visualise it absorbing any negative energy or emotions that you wish to release.

5. Anoint the candle with citrus oil, starting at the wick and moving downward. As you do this, visualise any negative energy or emotions being purified and released, and being replaced by positivity and joy.

6. Place the clear quartz on the altar or nearby.

7. Light the candle and recite the following incantation:

By the power of the elements and the light of the sun, I call upon the energies of positivity and joy. Let all negativity be dissipated and let only positivity remain. With the help of the clear quartz and the rose petals, I invite love, joy, and positivity into my life. With the use of the citrus oil, I invite the energy of the sun to warm my heart and soul.

After the spell is cast, allow the candle to burn out completely and dispose of the used wax with respect and gratitude. Keep the clear quartz near you to continue absorbing negative energy and to keep the positivity spell active.

Protection from Psychic Attack

Items needed:

- White candle
- Sage or rosemary oil
- Matches or a lighter
- A piece of black tourmaline or haematite
- A small bowl of dried sage

Instructions:

1. Cleanse your space by smudging with sage or burning lavender.

2. Sit comfortably in front of the candle and ground yourself by taking a few deep breaths.

3. Create a protective circle by casting sage around the area where you will be performing the spell.

4. Hold the black tourmaline or haematite in your hand, and visualise it absorbing the energy of protection and grounding.

5. Anoint the candle with sage or rosemary oil, starting at the wick and moving downward. As you do this, visualise yourself surrounded by a protective shield, blocking any negative energy or psychic attacks.

6. Place the black tourmaline or haematite on the altar or nearby.

7. Light the candle and recite the following incantation:

By the power of the elements and the light of the moon, I call upon the energies of protection and grounding. With the help of the black tourmaline/haematite and the sage, I invite a shield of protection around me. With the use of sage/rosemary oil, I fortify my aura and block any negative energy or psychic attacks. I trust in the universe to guide and protect me.

After the spell is cast, allow the candle to burn out completely and dispose of the used wax with respect and gratitude. Keep the black tourmaline or haematite near you to continue absorbing the energy of protection and grounding.

Additionally, it's important to remember that psychic attacks are rare, and that most negative energy or feelings of insecurity come from within. By working on yourself, you can reduce the likelihood of feeling affected by any negative energy.

Protection

Items needed:

- One white candle for purification
- One blue candle for protection
- One black candle for banishing negative energy
- Herbs such as rosemary or sage for purification
- A protective symbol or object (such as a pentacle)

Instructions:

1. Begin by purifying your space. Light the white candle and waft the herbs around the area to clear any negative energy.

2. Next, light the blue candle and hold the protective symbol or object in your hands. Visualize a blue light surrounding you, providing protection and safety.

3. Finally, light the black candle and visualize any negative energy or harm being drawn into the candle and banishing it from your space.

4. As you continue to visualize, repeat the following incantation:

With the power of white for purification, Blue for protection, Black for banishing negativity, I call upon the elements and the divine, To surround and shield me, Granting me safety and peace.

Allow the candles to burn down completely, making sure to keep a close eye on them. When the spell is finished, dispose of the wax and herbs in a respectful manner.

Purification

Items needed:

- White candle
- Sage or lavender essential oil
- Matches or a lighter

Instructions:

1. Cleanse your space by smudging with sage or burning lavender.

2. Sit comfortably in front of the candle and ground yourself by taking a few deep breaths.

3. Anoint the candle with sage or lavender oil, starting at the wick and moving downward. As you do this, visualise any negative energy or emotions being purified and released.

4. Light the candle and recite the following incantation:

By the power of the elements and the light of the moon, I call upon the energies of purification and release. Let all negativity be dissipated and let only positivity remain. I cleanse my mind, body, and spirit.

Raise and Boost Energy

Items needed:

- Purple candle
- Frankincense or myrrh oil
- Matches or a lighter
- A piece of amethyst or purple fluorite
- A small bowl of dried frankincense resin

Instructions:

1. Cleanse your space by smudging with sage or burning lavender.

2. Sit comfortably in front of the candle and ground yourself by taking a few deep breaths.

3. Create a protective circle by casting frankincense resin around the area where you will be performing the spell.

4. Hold the amethyst or purple fluorite in your hand, and visualise it absorbing the energy of magical power and strength.

5. Anoint the candle with frankincense or myrrh oil, starting at the wick and moving downward. As you do this, visualise yourself becoming more powerful and confident in your magical abilities.

6. Place the amethyst or purple fluorite on the altar or nearby.

7. Light the candle and recite the following incantation:

By the power of the elements and the light of the stars, I call upon the energies of magical power and strength. With the help of the amethyst/purple fluorite and the frankincense, I invite a boost of power to guide me in my magical practice. With the use of frankincense/myrrh oil, I open my mind and senses to the magic within me. I trust in the universe to help me to harness my full potential.

After the spell is cast, allow the candle to burn out completely and dispose of the used wax with respect and gratitude. Keep the amethyst or purple fluorite near you to continue absorbing the energy of magical power and strength.

It's important to remember that this spell is not a replacement for daily practice of self-improvement and learning, such as studying different magical practices, developing your intuition, and learning about the correspondences of different elements and energies. Additionally, it is important to remember that true magical power comes from within, and it can be strengthened through self-discovery and understanding, rather than relying on external sources.

Relaxation

Items needed:

- White candle
- Chamomile oil
- Matches or a lighter
- A piece of rose quartz
- A small bowl of dried chamomile

Instructions:

1. Cleanse your space by smudging with sage or burning lavender.

2. Sit comfortably in front of the candle and ground yourself by taking a few deep breaths.

3. Create a protective circle by casting chamomile around the area where you will be performing the spell.

4. Hold the rose quartz in your hand, and visualise it bringing peace and tranquility to your body and mind.

5. Anoint the candle with chamomile oil, starting at the wick and moving downward. As you do this, visualise yourself relaxing and letting go of any tension or stress.

6. Place the rose quartz on the altar or nearby.

7. Light the candle and recite the following incantation:

By the power of the elements and the light of the moon, I call upon the energies of peace and tranquility. With the help of the rose quartz and the chamomile, I invite relaxation into my life. With the use of chamomile oil, I release tension and stress. I trust in the universe to guide me and support me in my journey to relaxation.

After the spell is cast, take some time to sit and meditate with the candle burning, focusing on your breath and visualising yourself becoming more and more relaxed. As the candle burns down, repeat the incantation in your mind as a reminder of your intention.

When the candle has burned out, take the rose quartz and carry it with you as a reminder of the intention you set during the spell. You can also add the dried chamomile to a sachet and place it under your pillow for continued relaxation during sleep.

Remember that the spell is a tool to help you focus your intentions and that true relaxation comes from within. Be patient with yourself and trust in the power of your own mind and body to bring you the relaxation that you seek.

Romance

Items needed:

- Red candle
- Ylang-ylang or patchouli oil
- Matches or a lighter
- A piece of garnet or red jasper
- A small bowl of rose petals

Instructions:

1. Cleanse your space by smudging with sage or burning lavender.

2. Sit comfortably in front of the candle and ground yourself by taking a few deep breaths.

3. Create a protective circle by casting rose petals around the area where you will be performing the spell.

4. Hold the garnet or red jasper in your hand, and visualise it absorbing the energy of love, passion and romance.

5. Anoint the candle with ylang-ylang or patchouli oil, starting at the wick and moving downward. As you do this, visualise yourself surrounded by love and passion.

6. Place the garnet or red jasper on the altar or nearby.

7. Light the candle and recite the following incantation:

By the power of the elements and the light of the sun, I call upon the energies of love, passion and romance. With the help of the garnet/red jasper and the rose petals, I invite love, passion and romance into my life. With the use of ylang-ylang/patchouli oil, I open my heart to receive love. I trust in the universe to bring me the love and passion that I need.

After the spell is cast, allow the candle to burn out completely and dispose of the used wax with respect and gratitude. Keep the garnet or red jasper near you to continue absorbing the energy of love, passion and romance.

It's important to remember that romance spell should not be used to control others or manipulate their feelings. The goal of this spell is to open yourself to the possibility of love, passion, and romance, not to force someone else to love you. Love should be given and received freely and with mutual respect and consent. Also, it's important to remember that this spell is not a quick fix, it will take time and effort on your part to manifest romance in your life. It's important to work on yourself, improve yourself, be kind and open to others and have a positive attitude towards love and romance.

Soothing, Calm, and Peaceful Sleep

Items needed:

- Purple candle
- Chamomile or lavender oil
- Matches or a lighter
- A piece of amethyst or moonstone
- A small bowl of dried chamomile flowers

Instructions:

1. Cleanse your space by smudging with sage or burning lavender.

2. Sit comfortably in front of the candle and ground yourself by taking a few deep breaths.

3. Create a protective circle by casting chamomile flowers around the area where you will be performing the spell.

4. Hold the amethyst or moonstone in your hand, and visualise it absorbing the energy of peaceful sleep and relaxation.

5. Anoint the candle with chamomile or lavender oil, starting at the wick and moving downward. As you do this, visualise yourself becoming relaxed and peaceful.

6. Place the amethyst or moonstone on the altar or nearby.

7. Light the candle and recite the following incantation:

By the power of the elements and the light of the stars, I call upon the energies of peaceful sleep and relaxation. With the help of the amethyst/moonstone and the chamomile flowers, I invite restful and rejuvenating sleep to guide me. With the use of chamomile/lavender oil, I calm my mind and body to receive the gift of sleep. I trust in the universe to help me to find peace and rest.

After the spell is cast, allow the candle to burn out completely and dispose of the used wax with respect and gratitude. Keep the amethyst or moonstone near you to continue absorbing the energy of peaceful sleep and relaxation.

It's important to remember that this spell is not a replacement for healthy sleep habits like sticking to a regular sleep schedule, and making sure your sleep environment is comfortable and conducive to sleep. Also, practising relaxation techniques like yoga or meditation can be helpful in promoting a peaceful sleep.

Spirit Contact

Items needed:

- White candle
- Sage or lavender oil
- Matches or a lighter
- A piece of clear quartz or selenite
- A small bowl of dried sage or lavender

Instructions:

1. Cleanse your space by smudging with sage or burning lavender.

2. Sit comfortably in front of the candle and ground yourself by taking a few deep breaths.

3. Create a protective circle by casting sage or lavender around the area where you will be performing the spell.

4. Hold the clear quartz or selenite in your hand, and visualise it amplifying your energy and helping you to communicate with spirits.

5. Anoint the candle with sage or lavender oil, starting at the wick and moving downward. As you do this, visualise yourself opening a communication channel with spirits.

6. Place the clear quartz or selenite on the altar or nearby.

7. Light the candle and recite the following incantation:

By the power of the elements and the light of the moon, I call upon the energies of communication and connection. With the help of the clear quartz/selenite and the sage/lavender, I invite spirits to come forward and communicate with me. With the use of sage/lavender oil, I open my mind and senses to the realm of the spirits. I trust in the universe to guide me and protect me in this communication.

It is important to remember that after the spell is cast, it is important to be open and receptive to any communication that may occur, and to have a way to end the communication when you are finished, such as saying thank you and closing the circle. Keep the clear quartz or selenite near you to continue amplifying your energy and helping you to communicate with spirits.

Success

Items needed:

- Yellow candle
- Lemon or ginger oil
- Matches or a lighter
- A piece of tiger's eye or carnelian
- A small bowl of dried rose petals or bay leaves

1. Cleanse your space by smudging with sage or burning lavender.

2. Sit comfortably in front of the candle and ground yourself by taking a few deep breaths.

3. Create a protective circle by casting rose petals or bay leaves around the area where you will be performing the spell.

4. Hold the tiger's eye or carnelian in your hand, and visualise it bringing clarity and focus to your endeavours.

5. Anoint the candle with lemon or ginger oil, starting at the wick and moving downward. As you do this, visualise yourself manifesting success in your endeavours.

6. Place the tiger's eye or carnelian on the altar or nearby.

7. Light the candle and recite the following incantation:

By the power of the elements and the light of the sun, I call upon the energies of success and achievement. With the help of the tiger's eye/carnelian and the rose petals/bay leaves, I invite success and prosperity in my endeavours. With the use of lemon/ginger oil, I open my mind and senses to the opportunities for success. I trust in the universe to guide me and support me in my goals.

It is important to remember that after the spell is cast, it is important to be open and receptive to any opportunities that may arise, and to have a plan to make use of any success that may come your way. Keep the tiger's eye or carnelian near you to continue bringing clarity and focus to your endeavours.

Also, it's important to remember that true success comes from within and it can be strengthened through self-discovery and understanding, rather than relying on external sources.

Wealth

Items needed:

- Green candle
- Patchouli or cinnamon oil
- Matches or a lighter
- A piece of pyrite or citrine
- A small bowl of dried basil or mint

Instructions:

1. Cleanse your space by smudging with sage or burning lavender.

2. Sit comfortably in front of the candle and ground yourself by taking a few deep breaths.

3. Create a protective circle by casting basil or mint around the area where you will be performing the spell.

4. Hold the pyrite or citrine in your hand, and visualise it amplifying your energy and attracting wealth to you.

5. Anoint the candle with patchouli or cinnamon oil, starting at the wick and moving downward. As you do this, visualise yourself opening a channel for wealth to flow into your life.

6. Place the pyrite or citrine on the altar or nearby.

7. Light the candle and recite the following incantation:

By the power of the elements and the light of the sun, I call upon the energies of abundance and wealth. With the help of the pyrite/citrine and the basil/ mint, I invite prosperity and financial abundance into my life. With the use of patchouli/cinnamon oil, I open my mind and senses to the flow of wealth. I trust in the universe to guide me and provide for me.

It is important to remember that after the spell is cast, it is important to be open and receptive to any opportunities that may arise, and to have a plan to make use of any wealth that may come your way. Keep the pyrite or citrine near you to continue amplifying your energy and attracting wealth.

www.ingramcontent.com/pod-product-compliance
Lightning Source LLC
Chambersburg PA
CBHW031342040426
42443CB00006B/436